CrossWords

A Weekly Devotional With
Prayerful Reflections and Encouraging
Thoughts

Pray on!

Mark

Mark Phillips

DEDICATION

I dedicate this book to Debbie, my wife. Debbie, if you ever need a heart transplant, I'll give you mine so that you can feel my love for you with every beat of my heart.

Thank you for showing me what it looks like to love God with all your heart, soul, and mind. I've seen Jesus in you!

CONTENTS

ACKNOWLEDGMENTS

I wish to thank my friend, Jody Holland, for his support and encouragement. Thank you to my family. I love you all. Thanks to the many friends who encouraged me to complete this project. Most of all, I thank Jesus. It is because of what He did for me on a cross that now, I have words.

The Beginning

I am not so naive as to assume every reader of this book will read the introduction. I do assume that some are so eager to "get into it" that they simply skip over the intro and dive in to the devotionals. The fact that you are reading this and I am writing this says to me that, perhaps there is something of importance for me to write and equally for you to read. So, here we go.

My journey started fairly normal but it took a turn that brought me to this place. When I was young, my calling was and still is to be in ministry. I assumed this would be with a traditional church role. I started in ministry as a youth minister, made my way through seminary, and found myself at a fantastic church as an associate minister. I was married to the love of my life, had two small girls, and a loving family in both my home and my church. Things changed when I was riding my dirt-bike with friends from church. A jump that I had made a number of times before went wrong and I went over the handlebars. My head hit just right to cause a traumatic brain injury which landed me in a coma in the hospital in Abilene, Texas.

What happened after that was a very long recovery and lots of rehabilitation. I had to learn to walk again, talk again, and regain control over my motor skills. As a part of my rehabilitation, I began working with wood and purchased my first lathe. God has an amazing way of seeing so far into the future as to know what another soul will need and how he can use an injured pastor to bring hope and healing to others. For years, I turned pens, made crosses, and learned to create something beautiful out of an old tree, an antler, or just about anything that was no longer in its original state. I had no idea this would be the very calling for which God would use me today. As I am writing this, the verse from my friend and mentor, Dr. Lewis Holland, just came in via text. It is Colossians 3:17, "An whatever you do, whether in word or deed, do it all in the name of the Lord Jesus, giving thanks to God the Father through Him."

My simple act of making holding crosses and sharing with others the truth of God's love has become my ministry. It is in action that we find purpose. I would like to say that I have never been down, or bitter, or wondered why God allowed my accident, my cancer, and my other struggles to happen. I have been taught that it is wrong to lie and there is no freedom in a lie anyways. Throughout each of the trials I have faced in my life, I have clung to my Lord and to the promise that was given us through His sacrifice. The crosses came about from an experience I had after I had already stepped onto God's path for my life to minister through woodworking. I went from making pens and crosses to hang on the wall to following a path of sharing God's love through "holding crosses." It was in mixing prayers with crosses and sharing God's love that I have found the purpose for my life in Christ now.

Some years ago, as I volunteered at a church hospital visitation ministry team, a pastor who knew of my woodworking told me about a fellow woodworker in the Dallas area who made crosses to hold. My first thought and question was, "Cool, but can't all crosses be held?" "Yes," my friend answered, "but just look at them for yourself and see if it is something you would want to do to give to people as a prayer and encouragement tool."

I soon flew to Dallas to see how the crosses were made. I learned the technique and it wasn't very long before I made one for myself. I took it with me as I went to the cancer treatment center for chemotherapy. I needed something to hold onto, to remember to be faithful and to remember that I was not alone. This really helped me get through a very tough time. Now, I make these in a modified form and share them with others who need to know they are not alone.

That cross was the visual through prayer that connected me to the "real" power source, God. I have seen firsthand how a cross and an encouraging word can be used by God to help a person who is hurting, scared, confused, or feeling alone. It is from this knowledge that I write the following pages. My directive to both myself and to you is…

Pray On!

Mark Phillips

Week 1
An Engraver's Cross

I stopped by my engraver's office to pick up an engraving order. Noticing a few prayer crosses in my console, I grabbed one to show him. While I was in his office, I decided to give a cross to the engraver's assistant. I explained the cross and the meaning it has. Once I had shared of God's love and how the cross reminds us that we are never alone. She began to cry. She said, "Mark, I really needed this. See, my sister was killed in a terrible car crash a few weeks ago and I've been mad at God. I thought He didn't love me or care about me. Thank you for this cross. I needed this."

We spend so much of our time thinking that sharing God's love has to be formal, or at church, or that is bigger than we are capable of accomplishing. It isn't. Sharing God's love is in paying attention to God's tug on your heart to share a small gift, a word of encouragement, or to simply remind people that they are not alone. You never know when or how God can use you !

My challenge to you is to simply let someone know that they are not alone this week. Let them know that God is ever-present in their time of need. Listen to God, and... Pray On!

My Reflections…

Week 2
A Diner And A Cross

Today, I took my mother-in-law to some appointments she had and while out, we stopped at a favorite diner of hers. She asked the hostess to be seated in her favorite server's section. We had been there before, so we had developed a friendship with this server. In the course of our conversation, she told me of her sister who had advanced cancer. I shared with her how God had healed me of cancer. I remembered that I had a prayer cross in my jacket pocket. I handed it to her and told her to give it to her sister to hold as she goes for treatments. Our server gave me a hug as she fought back tears. She expressed her thanks as she held this cross. God is good! Will you join me in praying for all who battle cancer?

This week, my challenge to you is to pray daily for all of those who are fighting cancer. So many families are impacted by this disease, but they are not alone. Remind those who are in struggle that even though they may be in a battle, the great warrior is with them. Pray for those who are fighting for their health. Remember…. Pray On!

My Reflections…

Week 3
The Power In The Process

Every wooden cross has to go through a process of cutting, sanding, and finishing. I'm sure if wood could talk, it'd tell of how uncomfortable this process is. But as the crafter, I know what the finished piece will be. The process is necessary for the finished product. Isn't that true for us as well? As God shapes, cuts away the rough edges, and smooths us, the process may be uncomfortable. We may even desire that He be more "easy" with us. But as The Master Crafter, He knows what it takes to get us to the finished state. He knows that if a step is skipped, the end result will not be achieved. A popular motto from a long-standing 12-Step program says, "Let go and let God." That is applicable here. Let go and let God shape you. He knows the end result. His "shaping" has purpose and meaning (Jer.29:11).

My challenge to you this week is to seek God's shaping in your life. Do not seek ways to see the flaws in others, but rather allow God to do His master-work for you and for them. We are called to love as God loves. Seek God's shaping and allow God to transform you into all that He intended for you to be. And remember... Pray On!

My Reflections…

Week 4
Seeing God on Aisle Seven

God amazes me how He "sets up" encounters with others to encourage them with prayer crosses. While I was at the grocery store not too long ago, I noticed an older woman shelving items about halfway down the aisle. As I passed, I said, "Hello, Ma'am. How are you ?" She answered, "Well, I'm okay , if my husband could get better, we'd both be doing great." Stopping, I inquired, "Oh, what's the trouble?" She looked down, stepped off the stool she'd been on and related her story of caring for her husband in their home. She spoke of challenges to balance taking care of her husband while also working for needed income. I sensed her frustration. I even saw it in her eyes. I pulled out a prayer cross and gave it to her, encouraging her to place her concerns at the Lord's feet. She gratefully held the cross, looking up as if looking toward Heaven, and thanked me.

I haven't seen her in the store since, but I continue to pray for her. I pray she has seen God move in her life as she holds that cross and turns to Him. I saw God on aisle seven that evening! My challenge to you this week is to seek God no matter where you are. Seek ways to share His love by simply being willing to listen when another person is hurting. God sets up opportunities for us to share His love and his presence. You can find God anywhere and everywhere, even aisle seven. Always remember… Pray On!

My Reflections…

Week 5
The Cross… Your Story?

I was interviewed recently by a woman with a PR firm doing work for the Cancer Treatment Center in Atlanta about the ministry training I attended. In our conversation, she asked more about my own journey of recovery from my motorcycle accident (see introduction) and also cancer. I shared with her how God was opening up ways for me to share His love and encouragement through woodworking, especially prayer crosses. She ended up asking for mine and Debbie's book that told the story of my motorcycle accident and recovery, as well as a couple of crosses. Later, she texted appreciation for the crosses. She said how she was going to use her cross now and keep her infant son's cross in a safe place until he was older. She said that she'd put it up and share this later as it was "a part of his story." That got me to thinking how profound it is to think about the cross as part "of one's story". I want it to be part my story. Isn't the cross part of each person's "story"?

My challenge to you this week is to seek ways to make the cross a part of your story.

Never forget the sacrifice that was made so that you could experience the grace and forgiveness of God's love. And remember, Pray on!

My Reflections…

Week 6
The Cross… Is It Important To You?

God blessed me with another story that both encourages and challenges me. A nurse in Dallas who had me make something for her father told me how much he loved the gift and that he had it close to him in his last days on earth. It warmed my heart to hear how much he enjoyed it and to ponder how much it meant to him. It raised a question for me.

What is truly most important to me? My pickup? Money? Other things? People? How important is the cross to me? Not just for a piece of jewelry, but does it represent life to me? Does my life reflect Christ and the life He gives by what He did on the cross? How that man felt in his last days, the peace he experienced, are what I strive for each day.

Maya Angelou said, "People will forget what you said, people will forget what you did, but people will never forget how you made them feel."

My challenge to you this week is to seek ways to share God's love in order to help others feel at peace. And remember, Pray On!

My Reflections…

Week 7
Walk By Prayer

One of the first times I displayed crosses at a craft show was a few years ago in Hereford, Tx. After looking at several crosses, a lady picked out one and then told me she would hold it as she walked each morning and as she did, she would pray for her neighbors. My first thought was, "What a good neighbor to have- a praying one!".

In our day of people simply driving into their garages and closing off the rest of the world, we need more neighbors who pray and who care. Our world is too full of anger, violence, and hurtful intentions toward one another. We are the hands and feet for Christ. Just like the woman who is praying for her neighbors each morning as she holds her cross on her walk, we can pray for love to prevail. We can pray for those who may or may not even know who we are. That is my challenge to you this week. Pray for your neighbors. Pray for good in their lives. Pray for them to experience the grace and peace of Christ. And always remember, Pray On!

My Reflections...

Week 8
The Cross… Shape Me, Lord

I am sitting on our front porch this morning finishing some black walnut prayer crosses. As I sand them smooth, I'm reminded of how I need my Lord to "sand" me - to remove the rough places, impurities, undesired parts. Do you need Him to do some sanding" on you too? The difference between the wood and us is that the wood has no choice. It is at the mercy of the craftsman. You and me? We can choose to ask the Master Craftsman to do His work . If we do, the finished work will be worth all of the sanding.

Your life is yours. God is standing at the door of your heart and knocking. The difference between Christianity and other religions is that God is seeking you. He wants to invest in His craftsmanship, His work, His love in your life. He is seeking ways to sand you and shape you into the best version of you possible. My challenge to you this week is to ask God to shape you into a representation of His love. And always remember… Pray On !

My Reflections…

Week 9
An Intentional Moment

I went inside one of my favorite places to eat today and as I did, the general manager saw me and greeted me. I first met her in a business networking group led by my friend Jody. This GM knew bits of my story and how God had opened up a new ministry for me with woodworking. I told her about these prayer crosses. She said how she wanted to get her fiancé and a few others one too. I asked her how many she wanted and she looked up as many do while doing math "in their head" and sheepishly said, "Maybe 5." By the questioning inflection in her voice tone, I think she did not know I regularly keep some in my pickup's console, because you just never know...

I went out to my truck and counted my "stash" of crosses, and I had exactly 5! I re-entered the restaurant and gave them to her, and she said, "Wow, God knew these were for me, huh? I'm having a bummer of a day and you don't know how I needed to hear/see God now".

I don't believe in "karma" or "luck". I believe for the Christ-follower, that there is intentionality to our lives. Jeremiah 29:11 says that God has plans and purpose for us. The Psalmist said in Psalm 139 that all our days on earth are known by Him. Therefore, this "being in the right place at the right time " should be replaced with the words of Psalm 37 where we are reminded that God "orders" the steps of the righteous. As we live for Him by His word, we can rest assured that we can be in the right place at the right time !

For me, that "right time" was today at a restaurant in Amarillo, Texas, giving someone who was having a bad day some wooden prayer crosses. These crosses were something to remind them that God is here and He cares.

My challenge to you is to allow God to intervene in your life. When you listen to God's urging to demonstrate His love to others, he arranges the opportunities. He has a purpose for you. His purpose for your life, though, is dependent upon you allowing Him to work in your life. It is dependent upon you acting on God's urge to show love to others. Always remember… Pray on !

My Reflections…

Week 10
Taking A Cross To A Clothes Closet

For several years, I have spent Friday mornings at a clothes closet in northeast Amarillo with about a dozen others giving used clothing to people in need. I have seen the Lord in this space many times, including today. I pulled up to a parking spot with the already-formed line in front of me and I reached for a walnut prayer cross. Honestly, I'm thinking, "I'll take this one with me, but I doubt I'll be giving one out here."

I walked over to the line of folks there. As I did, a woman I had seen here before walked toward me and asked, "Hey, preacher, what happened to your leg?" Now, I'd like to tell you that my immediate thought was "Yes, Lord. I have another opportunity to tell someone that my limp is a residual sign of my near-death accident and how You healed me." Truth is, I was thinking that this was an inconvenience and she didn't seem to be a person who'd be interested in prayer anyway. Well, I went ahead and told her a bullet point version of a long story. Motorcycle accident. 2 weeks in a coma. Months in hospital. Discharged in a wheel chair. Semi-paralyzed on left side. Took up working with wood as therapy. Cancer 7 years later. Now I make crosses to encourage and inspire others. I do a prayer cross to remind of God's presence. To my surprise, she excitedly asked, "Oh, do you have one of those prayer crosses with you? I'd like one. I'm thinking, "O.K. Lord .., I hear ya'!"

Sorry if you want to hear/see some deep theological ponderings from a perfectly-focused with no weaknesses "man of the cloth." What you get here today is an honest admission from a far-from-perfect preacher with a limp that when I got to the clothes closet today, I was terribly amiss to think who needed/wanted a prayer cross. Thank You, Lord, for reminding me that we ALL need the cross. Like the gospel singer of old sang, we all are "standing in the need of prayer!" That woman's smile was the "proof in the pudding" for me. She gladly exclaimed as she clutched that little cross close to her heart, "Thank you, thank you, I'll carry this with me everywhere!"

No, Lord, Thank You, for this opportunity to see that Your grace is for us all. Bless this woman who came for clothes but left with a garment of praise in her heart as she held this prayer cross.

My challenge to you is the same challenge the Lord gave to me. Look for ways to show grace and share love this week. Let go of having to know the answer and allow God to guide you where He needs you. And always remember... Pray on!

My Reflections...

Week 11

A CrossWords thought on Mothers...

I started a non-profit in 2016, called OvercomerNow. The mission of this organization is to share information with others in order to inspire them to live a better life in Christ. I did not think about my prayer crosses as a part of the mission originally because the focus was on bringing in speakers to the Amarillo area, which we still do. God showed me very quickly that in order to overcome any challenge, we need to cling to the cross. Sometimes that realization of what I have needed in my life as an overcomer has been given to me by my Heavenly Father.

As I sit holding my own OvercomerNow prayer cross, I am reminded of a song by Rich Mullins titled, " Hold me, Jesus." Are you like me and sometimes you just want Jesus to hold you, like a momma holds her baby ? You just need to feel His heartbeat up against you. Draw near to Him in prayer, not asking for anything. Just come near to Him and just "be" in that moment. May we rest in His love and know that He will at times calm the storm. Other times, He'll calm the child!

My challenge to you this week is to allow God to hold you and love you. In a world where people seemed to struggle with keeping up with their neighbors and often feel they are not enough, remember that God loves you as you are. He loves you and sees your beauty and perfection in the same way a mother sees her child's perfection. Allow God to love you this week. Never forget… Pray on!

My Reflections...

Week 12
Simple Function

As I got in my pickup this morning, I did a quick visual inventory of my console. After noting that my prayer cross supply was getting low, I started thinking about my console, it's use and function. It pretty much has to deal with whatever I put there, be it a cup of coffee in the cup holder or a receipt in the tray where I keep crosses. Our lives have "consoles" too... our heart. The "console" of the heart holds things we hold dear like relationships with those close to us. This console can also hold things not so good, like past hurts or unforgiveness.

After a while, the console needs cleaning - both in your vehicle and in your heart. Not doing so allows things to take root and left there long enough, will cause great damage to that console. When I look at my console with crosses sitting and waiting to fulfill God's purpose, they remind me it is there, at the cross, we find the One who, because of what He did on the cross, can cleanse our "consoles" or hearts.

My challenge to you this week is to allow God's grace in your life and in your heart. Let God clean out your console of any hurt or unforgiveness. When you forgive others, it is as much for you as it is for them. I am thankful that God cleans out my heart regularly and keeps me on the right path. Be forgiving and… Pray on!

My Reflections…

Week 13
Deja-Cross

I went to Walgreens for some medicine. A woman was at the counter to ring up my purchase. I reached in my pants pocket for my card and I didn't feel it, but I found - six bucks, some coins, my pocket knife, and a prayer cross. Searching my other pocket for my debit card, I found it.

While "unloading" my pocket contents on her counter, the employee commented on my cross. She said, "Oh, I see your cross is different than the one you gave me. I just love mine. I've come across mine many times and it seems like it is just at the time that I need reminding of the Lord and His presence." At this point, I'm thinking, "My bad. I forgot I had even given her a cross". How about you? Have you ever done something for another person and forgot you had done the act? Not that it wasn't important, but your automatic response was to do something with no hidden agenda, nothing expected in return. I think God's "up" for us doing that. Yes, I think He loves it when His children just do things because it's right. It's loving. It's what He'd do.

My challenge to you for this week is to be loving to others with nothing expected in return. Simply demonstrate the love of Christ to your family, your friends, and even strangers. Pray On !

My Reflections...

Week 14
Pentecost Sunday

Although it may not be Pentecost Sunday when you are reading this, that is the day that I am writing this. It's a beautiful Sunday evening on Pentecost Sunday as I sand and apply some finish to some black walnut prayer crosses here on my front porch. We had a wonderful worship service today, remembering the power and work of the Holy Spirit.

The finish I am rubbing into these crosses helps me think of God's Spirit "finishing" me. His work protects me. It fills in the cracks and low places. All things this finish does to these crosses I am working on .

All of my crosses have been worked on by hand with the finish I have been talking about. Why not take a moment next time you pray to thank God for the "finishing" work of His Spirit just as the cross you then hold has been finished and protected too. That is my challenge for this week. Allow God to be the master craftsman and to polish you into the beautiful soul he sees. Allow him to wash over you with His love and His forgiveness.

He already sees your perfection. Allow Him to show it to you as well. As always… Pray On !

My Reflections…

Week 15
Taco Tuesday

My family went to eat tonight after our granddaughter's Spring band concert. We enjoyed the music of the 6th- 8th grade students of her school. Right before the last song, the director announced the winner of a memorial scholarship to attend a local university band camp this summer. Our granddaughter had entered her essay and we were hopeful. The director finally announced the winner as our granddaughter . We were so excited.

After the concert, we decided to partake in "Taco Tuesday." Talk about an awesome night! I was with my family, my granddaughter had won the award, and we had tacos! Somebody pinch me!

Standing last in our family in the serving line, I gave the cashier my order. She commented on my cross necklace. "Wow, how beautiful. Do you make them" she asked. I said "yes" and that I also make prayer crosses too. "Oh yeah," she said, "what do they look like?"

I reached in my pocket not knowing for sure if I had one. Fumbling through my coins, a gum wrapper, and something that I'm not sure what it was, I found a little prayer cross and handed it to her.

She was overjoyed. I wonder if we, Christ followers, ought to have an "Encouragement Tuesday" or a "Share God's love Wednesday." How about simply being "Excited to know and love Jesus" everyday as we pray the price and encourage others? I'm thankful for Taco Tuesday because it offered me another day to share the love of God with someone who needed to feel His presence.

My challenge to you this week is to wake each day and be thankful that God seeks you out every day. Be thankful that you are loved, cared for, and saved by grace. Simply show gratitude this week for His love, and remember... Pray on!

My Reflections...

Week 16
A Reminder

In my opinion, Post-It notes rank up there with roller wheels on big luggage and Velcro on kids' shoes. They are AWESOME!

Reaching inside my pant pocket for the money I had to purchase a new supply of those clever and sticky reminders, I felt my prayer cross. Immediately, a thought came to me. These prayer crosses are the post-it notes that remind me of God's love in my life. Each time I cling to a prayer cross, it reminds me of the times He has come near to me in my prayer time. It reminds me of some of the prayers prayed while holding it.

Isn't that something Post-It notes are used for…reminders? Reminders are good. They help us stay focused. In that sense, what better Post-It note is there than the cross? I like what Paul said about focus, "I've got my eye on the goal where You are calling me onward (to Jesus). I'm off and running, and I'm not turning back now." Phil.3:14, The Message.

This week, I challenge you to cling to the love that God has for you in Christ Jesus and seek out people who need to be reminded that they are loved. We are called to serve as God's Post-It note, or reminder that He is ever present in both times of trouble and in times of plenty. Remind people that they are loved, and… Pray On!

My Reflections…

Week 17
A Memorial Day Cross

This is the Sunday before Memorial Day as I am writing this. It is the day set aside to remember those who sacrificed their life in service for our country. It is often the sacrifice of another person that makes our life possible. Those in the military that protect and preserve freedom help to ensure our American way of life gets to continue. It is easy, at times, to take for granted the freedom we have to worship a risen King in America. When I hold one of my crosses, I praise God for this freedom.

I have many holding/prayer crosses. Although the materials used in them are beautiful, I try remember that they represent/memorialize the greatest sacrifice ever, Jesus' death on the cross. Because of that, you and I can live eternally with Him. When you hold your cross, let it draw you to the One who gave His life for you. In so doing, you bring honor to whom it truly is due.

My challenge to you this week is to pay attention to the freedoms that you enjoy in this great country as well as in Christ. Every day of the year is the perfect day to memorialize the sacrifice Jesus made for us. Greet each day with a thankful heart and remember... Pray On!

My Reflections...

Week 18
CrossWords History

A little background ... I first became familiar with these little crosses when I was doing some visitation for a church here in Amarillo. A friend knew I enjoyed woodworking and loved to pray for others and showed me some holding crosses made by a man in Frisco, Texas. I contacted that man and flew to his shop to learn the technique. The first one I made was for a friend from Canadian, Texas, Bill Popham. He was a patient at a hospital in Amarillo. After visiting him, I left it with him just to hold and be reminded of God's presence. I encouraged him to use it to help him focus his prayers.

Since that initial visit to see Bill, I have given out so many I can't give an exact number. I try to remind recipients that there is no power inherent in these crosses. The power, of course, is in to Whom we connect. These are just visuals God can use to draw us in.

Recently, a friend saw how this ministry was growing and how it blessed others, and wanted to know how they could give money for the cost of materials . It was not my original intent to get money from others for this ministry, but isn't that how God works. He works continuously behind the scenes to set up what His purpose is for our lives. Being introduced to the holding cross, learning the technique from the guy in Frisco, and then sharing God's love was a part of God's plan for my life.

My challenge to you this week is to open your heart and your mind to God's master plan for you. Quite often, the plan is revealed in the little coincidences arranged before we even arrived on the scene. Start each day this week with letting God know you are open and ready to receive direction, and... Pray On!

My Reflections…

Week 19
A Grocery Story CrossWords

Yesterday, at a local grocery store, a young man had bagged my items, put them in a cart and then asked where I was parked. We made small talk about how hot it has been as we made our way to my pickup. I saw his name badge showed "Michael" on it.

Michael said he was enjoying his summer break from college classes. We felt the engulfing 90 Plus degrees heat upon leaving the building. God's Holy "Nudger" was already working on me. Michael was doing a good thing, taking my bagged groceries to my vehicle. I plunged my right hand into my pocket finding the 3 or 4 dollars I had. As Michael put the last bag in, I handed him those singles. He gratefully said, "Thank you." Instantly, the Holy One nudged me. He said, "Nope. Check the other pocket." Obediently, I did and found a prayer cross. Handing it to Michael caused an even greater joy than the aforementioned dollars. He said, "Wow, man, thanks. This is cool." All I could say was "You're welcome." "All of us need to be reminded that we always have God with us. Let this cross do that for you." "I will", said

Michael. "Thanks."

I thank God for this moment. Be reminded that everyone is "up" for encouragement and a reminder by our words and actions that God is always with us. My challenge to you is to find someone to encourage and to remind that they are loved. Pray on!

My Reflections…

Week 20
The Other Side of Adversity

Many of my crosses are regularly given to people going through some kind of ordeal or set back. What many of those people are seeking is a way to stay strong and focused on overcoming the challenge. I love the message conveyed in the word "resilience." I'm reminded of the Psalmist's words in Psalm 23 when he said "even though I walk through the valley of the shadow of Death".... "Through" not "live in" or "wallow" or "exist" but "through". Because of the work of Christ on the cross we can be assured that we, too, can "thrive amidst adversity" as the Lord walks us through the valley.

Think about the times you have had to walk through the valley. For many people, it feels as if the valley might not ever end. It is in remembering that Christ is beside you in the valley, guiding you to the other side, that you can find the hope and the peace you need. You are never alone in the valley and if there was a beginning, then there must be an end to the valley.

Friend, draw near to Christ through prayer when your "valley time" comes and He will provide all you need. My challenge to you this week is to spend time in prayer and connection with Christ. Stay focused on the truth that He is always with you and is guiding you through any trouble you might be facing. And as always… Pray on!

My Reflections...

Week 21
A CrossWords "Headline"

This just in ...

Though the headlines are not the story, they set the story up and announce it. There was a recent news story that a car full of preteens on their way to another friend's house for a sleepover was at a stoplight when another car pulled alongside it. The occupants in the second car, for an unknown reason, opened fire on the first car, striking some of the passengers. One of those was a boy named Jacobi.

As a result of this horrible act, Jacobi has been in a coma at Northwest Texas Hospital. An acquaintance asked me for holding crosses they could give to the boy's father and another for the boy as he emerges from the coma. These have been delivered to them. The symbolism of hope that is represented in the cross is often what we need in times of struggle and confusion. We cling to the Father in order to find our way out of the desperation of a situation. Even if the situation doesn't turn out the way we want it to or even if we are in a situation we never deserved to be in, like Jacobi, we can still hope.

Like a ship focusing on the lighthouse during a storm, holding on to the love of Christ during stormy times keeps us focused in the right direction. Holding onto a cross in prayer has allowed many people to navigate those stormy times to the safe harbor of God's presence. That is my challenge to you this week. Stay focused on the safe harbor that exists in keeping our focus on Christ. Hold on to His promises and His love. And never forget... Pray on!

My Reflections…

Week 22
A CrossWords Do-Over

In case there is any misunderstanding, let me clarify that this pastor is NOT perfect. This one is a vessel, like all Christ followers are charged to be, but this vessel has a few blemishes. This vessel has cracks. But I am encouraged to report that God has used me anyway, in spite of my weaknesses. His grace and mercy are astounding, aren't they?

The above was manifested yesterday as I returned to a local business and made a purchase. Two weeks ago, I was in that same store for another reason. When I was there, I saw an employee who rang up my purchase. I remember that this person had a brace on, covering part of the hand and wrist running a few inches up their arm. I remember making a remark that went something like , "I see you were in an argument with a difficult customer," or something lame like that. Their response caused embarrassment over my failed attempt to be funny, "No, I had a stroke."

I left the store that day with bagged item in hand. The Holy One was already nudging me that I missed an opportunity to encourage this person. "I should have given them a cross," I thought as I passed through the automatically opened door. When I was told they had suffered a stroke, I could have encouraged them with a prayer cross by saying, "On days when you don't feel like pressing on, hang on to this cross and pray to the One who can strengthen you."

My visit 14 days prior ended as I got back to my vehicle, I loaded my embarrassed self and said, "Lord, I'm sorry. I realize that I missed an opportunity to share encouragement and give a cross. If I ever see this person here again, I promise you, that I'll focus on You. I'll encourage them. I WILL give them a cross." By the way, if you ever promise God something, He may just "call you" on it!

Now two weeks have gone by since that visit. Yesterday, I saw this person in the same store, in the same spot within that store, same brace, different customer. Oh, it was me, again making a purchase, but I remembered what I had told God. After she rang up my item, I thought to myself, "Thank You, Lord." I reached for a cross in my pocket and handed it to her.

A face of appreciation then looked at me as she said, "Oh, thank you so much. I really needed this. I needed to hear you say that He hadn't forgotten me. Thank you."

This time, a reformed repeat customer left the store. Thank You Lord , for second chances and do-over's. My challenge to you this week is to be grateful for the second chances you are given by the Heavenly Father. Wake each day and thank Him for another chance to get it right and… Pray On!

My Reflections…

Week 23
Broken... A CrossWords Reflection

I have thought about and prayed over this entry a great deal because it touches my heart deeply. I have a small wooden box that was a gift to me from the pianist at the church I pastored in Kentucky. Inside the box was a hand written letter from my friend. She hoped that when I saw the box it would remind me of our Kentucky church family and the years we had there, and it has. This box, unfortunately, is a victim of being something belonging to a pastor who moves quite regularly. In its current broken condition, this box reminds me of something else too.

Isn't this box you and me? Broken? In need of a skilled hand to repair and possibly replace those broken pieces? The repair will take the time and tools of a craftsman. Our lives can, at times, seem or feel "broken" too.

When we are at this point, turn to the Master Repairman with experience / specialty in the area of "fixing" the broken. It'll take some time as He uses His "tools" of Scripture, worship, and prayer, but as you allow Him access to the "broken" areas, He'll make you strong again, new again. It might even be better than it was originally.

Friend, when you see a cross or hold your cross in prayer, thank Him for redeeming the "broken" and making them whole, wooden boxes and you and me. My challenge to you this week is to allow God access to the hurt you have been holding on to. Allow Him to be the master repairman of your life. Being healed begins with allowing God to love you and accepting that you are loved regardless of your condition. Always remember… Pray on!

My Reflections…

Week 24
What's Your Story?

Deb and I were picking up our grandkids' toys when I noticed some of their storybooks. We, like many, loved reading to our little ones. As I picked them up, the words of a song recorded by singer Collin Raye played in my mind. "That's My Story, and I'm sticking to it," he sang in the chorus.

I believe we each have a story, or as my friend Jody Holland points out, a "life word" that summarizes or encapsulates who we are and what we are about. Jody told me that as I discover my "life word," I'll discover that which I am most passionate about and the thing I find that rejuvenates me.

I hope as I position myself to live a life of faith, I'll discover that one of my "life words" is the cross. What is symbolized in the cross truly gives me life and rejuvenates me. I wonder if at my passing from this life to eternity, others who knew me would say that the cross was something that was seen in my life.

How about you? What's your story? What will be your life word? As you continue to pray on, is drawing near to the Father a part of you?

My challenge to you is to discover your calling in this life through Christ. Once you find it, be it prayer or witness or teaching or simply demonstrating God's love in your everyday actions, stick to it. May we do a version of Collin Raye's song to say, My Life Word... "That's My Story and I'm sticking to it!"

In your journey, always remember... Pray On!

My Reflections…

Week 25
An Idlewild CrossWords Reflection

One Father's Day, I spoke at the beautiful Idlewild Community Church just outside Eagle Nest, New Mexico. That was a sermon preached on Father's Day and the experience of sharing the gospel in that incredible place was truly amazing. First, I was with my very best friend, Debbie, in this truly magnificent setting, worshipping my awesome God with great people.

One of those great people was "Goose," the caretaker of the Idlewild property. While there, we had a tire blowout on our car. Goose tried to help us find a replacement, but after phone calls to a few mechanics in Eagle Nest, Red River, and even Taos, we had no leads on a replacement tire. Finally, we found one in Questa.

Goose helped me put the "donut" on and we were slowly on our way. With a bit of a delay, we finally got our replacement put on and eventually made it back to Amarillo. I'll not forget Goose's assistance and helpful spirit. I gave him a prayer cross while I was there simply as a reminder of my gratitude to him. I hope it reminds him not just of a preacher in need but also of the knowledge that God is ever present in our times of need. Sometimes He sends us a miracle who might have a cool name like, Goose.

When you draw near to God through prayer, no matter what the need at hand, you will ALWAYS be blessed by time with the Lord. My challenge to you is to take time to connect with God and allow him to send you help. We miss God's assistance because we are waiting on something that looks like a miracle instead of the miracle of someone simply showing us that they care. Allow God to love you, and… Pray On!

My Reflections...

Week 26
Enough

There is a small "resilience shelf sign" I make. It, along with prayer crosses and other handmade gifts are a part of the foundation I began known as OvercomerNow. These gifts are designed to help people remember that God is enough for all our trials.

As you continue in the faith journey to have a life of prayer, remember that God is truly enough, MORE than enough! Remember what God said to Moses when he asked who do I tell them (Israelites) it is that sends me? God said, "You tell them I am sends you" (Ex.3: 14). He is what? Everything. To the weary, He is rest. To the lonely, He is comfort. To the lost, He is direction. And on and on. He is everything. That's good to know! It is critical to embrace in any time of need.

Remember too, whose you are. You are a child of the great "I am." Like evangelist Ed Robb used to remind his kids, "Remember, you're a Robb." Remember my friend, you are a child of the Great "I am!"

My challenge to you this week is to end each day holding on to the feeling that you are loved and that God is enough to handle anything in your life with you. As you drift off to sleep each night, simply feel that God is enough, and… Pray On!

My Reflections…

Week 27
A Father's Day CrossWords

When I hold a prayer cross, I am reminded of that song, "He's Got The Whole World In His Hands." As a boy, a neighbor friend and I used to argue, "Well, my dad can whip yours," and on and on it'd go. Silly, yes. Childish, yes. Truthful, not sure because they never fought it out. But in my mind, my father was invincible. I'm pretty sure that somewhere between I-40 and Georgia Street, my dad went into a phone booth and took off his khakis every work day to put on his Superman clothes!

Fathers are like that to many of us, huh? Superhuman can do anything! Well, one thing you and I CAN be sure of... Our Heavenly Father CAN do anything! And as hard as it is to comprehend, He does, in fact, have the entire world, which He made by the way, in His hands.

Next time you pray, remember that you are speaking to the very one who holds you and us all in His hands. My challenge to you this week is to be thankful for the fathers we have on this earth and to remember that our

Father in Heaven is watching over us. He has each and every one of us in His hands. Feel safe in that knowledge and... Pray On!

My Reflections…

Week 28
A Dunaway CrossWords

I loved the years we lived in Kentucky when I was enrolled in Asbury Seminary. A big reason for this was the joy I had in pastoring Dunaway United Methodist Church outside of Winchester, Kentucky. Sandy Baker, a member of Dunaway, organized the children in a musical production, "The Donut Hole Gang."

Some words in the theme song of the donut hole gang were, "Life without God's love is like a donut... there's a hole in the middle of your heart." I have two prayer crosses that have the image of the dove cut out of them. This reminds me that to "cut out" or not allow the presence of God's Sprit in us makes us incomplete. Only God can fill that missing spot in our hearts.

Without God's love in us, we have something missing too. To some, we can "appear" okay, even functional on the outside, but as Sandy directed the Dunaway kids to sing, without Christ and His love, there's a "hole" in you, something missing on the inside, same for God's Spirit. Without the Spirit, there's something missing.

Too often, people will try to fill that hole in their heart and in their spirit with stuff. They obsess about life things instead of eternal things. While we are called to be good stewards of our time and resources on this earth, we are ultimately called to be in connection with the Father. This means that we must invite Him into our lives and allow Him to fill that empty space that only He can fill.

Friend, as you continue embracing the grace of prayer in your faith journey, may you remember to seek the Lord to be filled with His love in all you do. My challenge to you is to search your heart and find out if you have allowed God into all of you. Then, open up your spirit and ask Him to flood you, to wash over you, and to fill you with the peace that only He can bring, and... Pray On!

My Reflections…

Week 29
A "Porch Time" Reflection

It's Tuesday evening as I write this and I'm on my porch finish sanding and hand rubbing a sealer into some black walnut prayer crosses. The "hard" work of cutting them out has been done. Now comes the slower-paced part of sanding any rough places out and enhancing their intrinsic beauty by adding a finish to them.

This kind of makes me think of God's work in each of us. He takes time getting rid of the "rough" places and enhancing His presence in us, His Spirit. His Word tells us that He has plans… a design in mind for us (Jer.29:11) . That is one thing that encourages me in the time-consuming process of the finish work of making crosses. I envision how it will look after I am through and the sanding and finishing becomes invigorating.

I often wonder if God doesn't see the same thing in us. As He invests time and energy in sanding off the rough edges and polishing us up to reveal the beauty He has always seen, surely He must get excited. I would imagine He is invigorated by the process of helping one of His children become what He has always seen!

My challenge to you this week is to take a moment or two the next time you are praying and thank Him for taking His time "finishing" you, getting you closer to His design. As God does His masterwork in your life, remember… Pray On!

My Reflections…

Week 30
A CrossWords Reflectionzsky

Okay, for all you "type A's" who are, right now, tensing up because of what you read that, to you, appears to be a "typo," relax. I meant to spell the word that wayzsky. Recently, I left a cross with a couple of teen employees of a nation-wide sandwich franchise.

As has happened before, I wasn't planning to leave a cross. I really just planned on ordering a delicious sandwich and enjoying my meal. After ordering my sandwich, I was preparing to leave, when I "sensed" a nudge to put a cross on the counter and say, "Y'all ever feel like you are "alone" in this world? And in their late-teen wisdom, one of them said, "Hey, yeah. Like the other day." He didn't elaborate. So I said, when you feel like that, look at this cross and remember He said, "I will never leave you." To which he said in a Wayne's World-esque tone, "Cool. Thanks man." The other one saw the cross and her comment was, "Awe, that's cute." I wanted to say, "Cute? The cross, cute?" But I reigned in my theological desire to mandate the right interpretation. I realized that whether the cross is seen as cute or cool or totally rad or holy, the power that God has in this world is the same.

We are often tempted to try and demonstrate our superior intellect, or superior holiness to others. God doesn't need us to put people in their places. What the cross represents is a sacrifice that made eternal life possible. The cross is life! It's a symbol of the thing that God allowed His son to die on so that we would not just have life, we can have abundant life! I challenge you this week to remember that God has things in control. When we focus on living an abundant life, others are drawn to understand why. Each person may interpret the meaning of the cross in their own way. Some will think it is cool, others rad, some cute, and still others will say it is awesome. Rest in the assurance that God's power is not dependent on another person saying things in the right way. His power is eternal. So remember... Pray On!

My Reflections…

Week 31
From The Ford Dealership

I had taken my pickup in for service today when I noticed the lift in the garage. Most of us have seen them and probably had our vehicle lifted up by one for an oil change or a tire rotation. They aren't that new but they are incredibly handy for making the work to be done on our vehicle possible.

A thought came to me. I was reminded of an often used expression for praying, "lifting a concern up to the Lord." Pastor Ed Hampton at Faith Mountain Fellowship Church in Red River, New Mexico had me consider visualizing myself placing my concerns in my hands and lifting them up over my head and saying to God," Lord, here is (name the concern specifically). And continue, "I give it to You. My faith is in You. It's now in your hands." My friend Ed explained further, "Mark, when you give a concern to Him, give it. Exercise your faith. If He drops it or it's changed, then so be it. Prayer and faith are cousins. Let them do their work."

Thanks Ed for that teaching. I pass it on to you. As you continue to access the power of prayer, consider embracing prayer's cousin, faith, and let them tag team you or "lift" you as the lift did with my pickup today. Once lifted, the needed work can begin. My challenge to you is to allow God to lift you up when you pray and then allow the old things to be removed, just like a mechanic removes the parts that are broken. Finally, know that God will always put a healed spirit in you if you will allow Him. Allow God to lift you, and… Pray On !

My Reflections…

Week 32
A CrossWords Protect-flection

Today's thoughts are about a revolver, prayer crosses, and safety glasses. All can protect (hence, the "invented" word in the title, combo of protect and reflection). This sparks a couple thoughts.

First, most of us have prayed prayers of protection by asking God to take care of someone as they travel or are in transition to a new place. We ask God to "be with them," but do we need to ask that? The last thing Jesus said in human form is recorded in Matthew 28:20. It says that He'll not leave us and that He'd always be with us. Maybe we need to pray that we will be mindful of His presence. If we are not careful, we can let too many things get in the way of our chance to experience God.

Second, if you ever need ideas to spark prayers for protection, then turn to Psalm 25 or Psalm 91. I think God loves it when we pray His Word back to Him in faith. As you continue living a life of prayer in your faith journey, be thankful our God loves us so much that He protects us. God's love for us reminds me of my grandson and his obsessive love of Mickey Mouse. It's a known fact in our family that you just do not mess with his Mickey blanket. There's not much my grandson will not do for that blanket. He cherishes and loves it. You are infinitely more important to God than that blanket is to my grandson! He protects that which He loves! This week, my challenge is that you rest in the truth of God's protection over your soul. You are loved and your watched over. So remember... Pray On!

My Reflections...

Week 33
Be Prepared

One of my earliest times of sharing a small prayer cross was with a hotel employee in New Mexico as we traveled home from speaking at a prayer conference. One morning in the area where the complimentary breakfast was served, I began a "small talk" conversation with the clerk at the front desk. After exchanging the usual, where I was from, how many in the family, occupation, etc., she began sharing her story.

She told me how she and her family had been involved in a serious accident while returning home from being with her husband's parents in Oklahoma. While on the Interstate and with her at the wheel, she lost control of their car as she swerved to miss a piece of debris strewn on the road. The car flipped. She and their children survived with a few scratches and bruises. However, her husband incurred a skull fracture and he is now on disability. The remainder of her story centered around the difficulties of adjusting to a new way of life and also the damage done to her relationship with her in-laws who blame her for the accident and subsequent physical condition of her husband. She shared sensitive issues as much as being in a hotel lobby would allow. After I listened to her story, I prayed for her.

Since we were returning from having spoken in a church in Albuquerque, I had a few copies of our first book, <u>The Last Ride</u>, and some crosses in the car. Immediately, I went out and got a book and enough crosses for her entire family and gave them to her. I understood her frustration from a different angle. I have gone through so many things in this life and it can be overwhelming to adjust to the new normal.

I do not know if I'll ever see this person again. I DO know that if we ever pass through that city again, I'll pray for her and her family. This time further underscored for me the importance of being ready to share God's love and encouragement whenever I can. It is in hope and in keeping our focus on what Christ can do next that we find peace.

I challenge you to intercede for those who are hurting, those who have had life-altering accidents, and for those who simply need to reclaim hope. Pray that they may experience the love of God regardless of how their circumstances have changed. With all your heart, this week… Pray On!

My Reflections…

Week 34
A Kids' Version of Reflections

Debbie and I were present as one of my grandsons closed out his baseball season recently. Deb and I are so blessed to have our grandchildren. They each bring us great joy. I remember giving the three oldest grandkids a prayer cross. I told them why they were important and how they could be used to encourage others. My grandson asked me for an extra one because a boy in his neighborhood had been ill and he wanted to give him a cross to cheer him up. He did and it did. Prayer and encouragement mission accomplished!

We can easily become discouraged by school shootings, young people getting in trouble with law officers, etc. But, with actions like my grandson's, maybe there is some hope for us. His action also challenges us adults. If a kid could reach out to another, then why can't I do it and you too? "And a little child shall lead them." Isaiah 11:6.

We often overthink the world around us and overanalyze whether God would want us to try and help. My challenge to you this week is to simply listen with the heart of a child to God's tug on your life. Listen like a child and seek out ways to bring that kind of faith, hope, and love to the rest of the world. As children lead us to be better Christ followers... Pray On!

My Reflections…

Week 35
On The Run

I had returned for my now favorite drink, ice water with strawberry and lemon. At the drive up window, I saw the employee inside "craning" their neck to see me through the window. Quickly, that employee burst out a side entrance and ran up to my downed window. I recognized that I had given them a prayer cross two days earlier when I heard, "Oh, I'm so glad to see you. Someone took my cross out of my jacket. I'm so bummed. Can I get another one, please?"

I'm seeing the genuine feelings of sadness in her face and, at the same time, I'm reaching for a cross in my console. "Sure, here you go." "Oh wow, thank you so much!! I've got to get back inside now, but I'll get your water next time, okay?" I said," No worries. Glad to give it to you."

This is NOT about me giving another cross away. This incident reminds me of the days early in my faith journey when I'd be so excited about new things I discovered about the Lord. I'd get excited just to be with Him, just to pray. I saw a child-likeness in the young person today. Her sadness was easily reversed in a simple act. The recipient's behavior was simple, pure, and uncomplicated. I think God likes that stuff. Psalm 116:6 tells us, "The Lord preserves the simple."

There's purity in simple things. Have you lost that child-like, simple, pure, faith? Why not run to Him in prayer like the young person who ran to me today, and embrace Him like a child once again. My challenge to you is to practice living this week in awe of what God is doing in your world, and...Pray On!

My Reflections…

Week 36
Recommitment

I was looking at a picture taken at my wife and my 15th Anniversary "Recommitment of Vows" service. The first reason I like this memory is because of the obvious, being photographed with my beautiful Debbie. She makes me better than I could ever be on my own. The picture I am reflecting on is also important because it was taken a few months after my accident. I was still in a wheel chair. For this picture, she is holding me up. She has done this for me many, many, times emotionally and spiritually over the course of our marriage. Also, at the bottom of the picture are three prayer crosses. Absolutely nothing we do as a couple brings us together more than prayer. I love our prayer time together. When I listen to her praying, I learn more about the things that move Debbie's heart. Prayer time at meals is good, but it is when we are alone praying that we draw closer to God and one another.

Because I have been with her hundreds, even thousands of times praying, I can say she is the most faithful prayer warrior I know. Prayer is the glue of our covenant. Whether you are married or single, I challenge you this week to recommit yourself to prayer. For those who are married, pray with our spouse and ask for God's blessing and guidance on your life together. If you are single, pray for God's hand to be on your life and to be with anyone that you are in relationship with now or even in the future. I believe you will be amazed by the power of God in your life when you gather together and ask for His blessing. So never forget… Pray On!

My Reflections…

Week 37
Guitar Extraction

I was "thanked" by three different employees at a music store today for bringing in my acoustic guitar for an extraction of miscellaneous items placed in the sound hole. Apparently, they had done this before for other customers, just none blaming a 2 year-old grand-blessing.

After a few moments and as many laughs, extraction was successful. To get to this point, two strings had to be removed so the tech could squeeze his hand into my guitar. Believe it or not, a lesson "played" (a little music store humor) before me. I realized that sometimes things have to be removed in order for God's greatness to be revealed.

Like my friends who regularly lift weights have taught me, "You have to tear down before you build up." They are explaining why so much pain is felt in the beginning of an exercise program. Our muscles hurt a lot initially. I do not understand the physiology about this, I just know it's true because I hurt a lot at first any time I have tried to consistently exercise. It's like praying to God for a particular thing in your life. Sometimes, God has to do some deconstruction (might hurt at first) before He builds you back up or does the new work.

Don't be discouraged, my friend. Just as in weightlifting or the extraction of things a cute lil' grandson put in your guitar, the buildup WILL come! My challenge to you this week is to embrace the reshaping that God might be doing in your life. Lean in and let God build you up. And as always… Pray On!

My Reflections...

Week 38
Read Out Loud

My friend, Terry Teykl, is at it again - writing and publishing awesome prayer resources. You can see all of his titles at www.prayforrenewal.com.   I have been using my book, My Healing Devotional, every day since I received it. Editor, Lynn Ponder Moore, also the editor of our first book, wrote something powerful I want to share with you. Lynn encourages readers to read the prayers and declarations out loud. She says, "there's just something powerful about hearing affirmations and promises of God."

I agree that the spoken word has authority. Personally, when I speak these powerful things of God, it's like my faith becomes turbo charged. Let me piggyback another thought with Lynn's. One of the reasons I like using my prayer cross is that as I read God's promises, then speak them out loud, I add the sense of touch by squeezing the cross, and my experience is heightened.

I'd like to wholeheartedly encourage you to regularly use prayer resources as you continue to, as my friend Terry says, pray the

price. My challenge to you this week is to
spend time daily in prayer, but pray for others,
for God's Wisdom, for personal growth, etc.,
and pray out loud. There is power in the
spoken word. Practice here, by saying the last
words of this entry out loud… Pray On!

My Reflections…

Week 39
"Can't Miss It"

My friends, Gene and Connie, left Amarillo recently. At our last meeting, I gave Gene some of my prayer crosses. Gene and Connie are currently in South Dakota working as hosts at an RV park. This is the setting for which this amazing story of a little prayer cross emerges.

Gene told me there was a family from Wisconsin in the park. He learned that while there, the teen daughter of this family snuck off from her family's RV. It seems, the girl's boyfriend had come there in the dark of the night providing transportation for the duo to escape to Colorado.

Gene says camp video surveillance has been looked at but provides no proof the teen girl left under duress. Her parents were beyond worried. Gene told me that when he first learned of this, his knee-jerk reaction was to begin praying. He held onto a prayer cross praying throughout the day.

Later that same day, Gene saw the father of the girl who left her family. Gene told me that when he saw this heart-sickened man, in a "from one dad to another dad" moment, he told him how saddened he was to learn of what had happened. He knew they were concerned for their daughter. Gene spoke encouragingly of how he had been praying for them throughout the day.

Gene then pulls from his pocket the cross he had been holding. He encouraged the father to "Cling to the King," to lean on Him for strength. He also spoke of his prayers for the daughter, her safety, etc. I am certain it was a very moving moment when Gene then gave that cross to the father. In Gene's own words, the father teared up and then gave him a big 'ol bear hug!

Though that is the full story from Gene, there are many teachable "God things" for us here. We can focus on the "being in the right place at the right time" dynamic or the "power of prayer for protection" element. One thing for sure though, ALL who are reading this can pray for this family as well as others in crisis. The Father hears the prayers of His people. My challenge to you this week is to spend time daily in intercession for others. Prayer for protection. Pray for good choices. Pray for families to become whole again. In all things... Pray On!

My Reflections…

Week 40
Fishing

My granddaughter got a fishing "lesson" while at a nearby lake for July 4th festivities. She did well that evening catching multiple fish. After the darkened sky had been filled with colorful fireworks and we left the lake for the drive home, a prayer thought came to me in the car.

I can remember when I gave my life to Christ and invited Him into my heart. I recall trying to master "new" things that came with being a Christ-follower, like prayer. At first, I listened to my faith-filled leaders of the Tuesday night share and prayer group for youth at our church. They prayed with such ease, such eloquence. How could I ever be as good a pray-er as Margaret or Leo?

I listened more and began to read more Scripture. I began hanging out more with a cute girl named Debbie as well. I learned about Christ from her. The more I learned, the more I WANTED to pray. I just started taking action every day to deepen my walk with Christ. I think that God wants to see His people moving closer to Him. All He desires from us is a relationship. Every relationship requires effort in connecting. All of these thoughts and positive emotions were swirling around my mind and filling my heart with love.

My next thought was, thanks, Lord. Thank you for your goodness and mercy and most of all, for caring for a guy like me. As we continued driving home that night, God reminded me that praying is the best way to learn how to pray. Just like my granddaughter was learning to fish by fishing, each of us develops confidence in a new thing by practicing and acting in the right direction.

My challenge to you this week is to practice both prayer and connection with the Father. Don't worry about whether you are saying just the right words. Instead, spend time with God. Talk with God. Mostly, just take action, and... Pray On!

My Reflections...

Week 41
Burgers and Songs

Occasionally, I see a guy named Darryl at a local fast-food restaurant. From time to time, I grab a quick bite with Darryl and visit with him. You see, Darryl is homeless and has been for all the years I have known him. Usually, when he sees me or Deb or another member of our family, he'll come over to us and talk. He is quite the storyteller and singer. His songs are often woeful but sometimes humorous.

Darryl draws from his years of living on the streets in the downtown area of Amarillo as the inspiration for his stories and songs. We left the burger joint and got in my pickup so I could take him the few blocks to where he "lived" in an abandoned vehicle. Settling in for the relatively short commute, I phoned Deb so that Darryl could say hello. He wastes no time in asking if she'd like to hear a song. She did, so Darryl obliged. Debbie got a double treat though. Darryl sang her two songs!

It did not take very long at all to arrive at our destination, an abandoned van behind a business that Darryl made into a home . Right before he got out of my pickup though, he asked me If I remembered giving him a wooden cross a few months ago. I responded that I did. He went on to say, "When I see that, I wonder how you are doing." Being a preacher, I thought I should say something "preachy" so I said, "Well, Darryl, when you see that cross, I hope you remember that God loves you." His response one-up'd my words. He said, "Yup, I know He do. He sent you to the restaurant and I got to eat plus sing to your wife."

My challenge to you and to myself is to simply be kind to others in need. We often don't know their story. We do, however, know that God loves them and often sends us to share a little of that love with them on earth. Thank you Lord, for reminding me of the joys in burgers and songs. Be nice and... Pray On !

My Reflections…

Week 42
Ice Cream and Substitutes

Imagine going to your local ice cream parlor for your favorite flavored ice cream treat . The treat "architect" asks for your order and you tell him what you'd like. You then hear the two most devastating words on this treat retrieval excursion, "Sold out." Wh-wh-what did he say? Sold out? How could this happen? Call the local press. Inform the F.B.I. Someone, do something, and quick! We've got an emergency before us that might cause irreversible damage! Or, at least a minor inconvenience.

"Seriously, now, Phillips, pull yourself together" you might be thinking. And I did do just that. I wasn't too traumatized. I simply chose one of the other bazillion flavors. Once again, treat retrieval and enjoyment resumed! We often get bent out of shape over small things and forget the really important things. My friend Jody Holland has asked me before, "Are you having a bad day or are you having a bad 5 minutes and hanging onto it all day?" Too often, we let the little inconveniences of life take our attention away from what really matters the most. Christ died for the forgiveness of our sins. I would say that beats out making sure I have the right ice cream every single time.

When you think of the cross, be reminded of the love and sacrifice that God made in sending Jesus to this earth. Think of the love that Jesus demonstrated in being obedient and being the sacrifice for our sins. The only one, and I do mean the ONLY one who could do that, was Jesus. We should have paid our own debt of sin, but we could not and did not have to because of that love. God sent the ultimate "substitute," His Son, Jesus, to pay our debt for us. (see John 3:16,17).

I did survive the ice cream dilemma by taking advantage of a "substitute" flavor. Be reminded, friend, that it is because of the best "substitute" ever, Jesus, that we ALL survive the sin dilemma. My challenge to you this week is to maintain perspective. The little annoyances in our lives are nothing in comparison to the sacrifice that has been made for us. We are forgiven because He first sought out a way to forgive us. Never forget that you are loved, and... Pray On!

My Reflections...

Week 43
Gun Show

I think most reading these little devotionals know that one thing I began doing after my accident is working with wood and other materials to produce handmade pens, crosses, and other items. God has used this as therapy to regain use of my left hand in strengthening fine-motor skills. This is a testament to the recovery as seen in the picture of my hand on the front cover of this devotional book. Having made quite a few items, I began looking for the ideal place to sell the items and help support my family. A venue I discovered where many of my crafts have been well-received is at gun shows.

I recently had the chance to sell my pens and other items at a local gun show. I had some deer antler pens and rifle shell pens but directly in front of me, I had several prayer crosses. It was surprising to me that most passers-by commented on the crosses first. They seemed to catch the attention of the patrons more than other things. I loved that it was the cross that drew attention!

A person would pick up a cross and notice the unique design and ask about its meaning. I shared with them how I got involved making these. I told how others have used them and even offered up an idea or two on how they might use one. I tried to encourage people to not idolize that wooden cross and most would shake their head in agreement that this prayer cross just connected them to the REAL power source, the Lord.

You know what? Almost every time, people would tell me of a struggle they or someone else they knew had that would benefit from this visual prayer tool. I heard lots of stories that day. I even had the chance to pray for some of the folks at the show. It was awesome!

I was reminded of a scripture in Matthew 16 where Jesus said if we want to follow him, we must "take up our cross daily." For me, my cross this weekend was literally my prayer crosses at a gun show. Other times, following Christ meant taking up the cross of suffering for Him. Perhaps you are like me. A few years ago, I wouldn't have thought I could be at a gun show encouraging others and talking to them about prayer, but perhaps I needed to read that passage again. It does not say that taking up the cross of Christ is just for certain places or that other places are excluded.

My challenge to you this week is to ask the Lord where He wants you, where He needs you to go. As you take up your cross and follow Him, always, always… Pray On!

My Reflections…

Week 44
Signs

Amarillo has been under construction for quite some time now. Some would say that it seems like perpetual construction because almost every major street seems to be decorated with orange traffic cones. Everywhere a person turns, they seem to notice a "road construction ahead" or "detour" or "merge now" sign. Many city streets and even parts of the Interstate which pass through Amarillo are being populated with "detour" signs. I have friends that get particularly frustrated with having to reroute their normal pathways to get where they want to go.

Most of us do not like "detours." We are forced to consider alternate routes. This might even slow us down from our daily break-neck, multi-tasking-ism, way of living. Slowing down is a big part of being a follower of Christ though. It is in slowing down that we are able to recognize our need for God. It is also in the slowing down that we more clearly see what motivates us and what is truly important. When we slow down, even if we are forced to by some "detour," we can more clearly hear God.

I am reminded that in Psalm 46:10, we are told to "be still and know that He is God." Did you see the clear inference? It reads "be still," not "do still." I don't know about you, but I need to be reminded from time to time that I am a human "being", not a human "doing!"

Detours allow me to slow down and if a life "detour" comes in the form of bad health or other setback, I am forced to just "be", not "do." My challenge to you is to ask God what "detour" He is allowing in your life to slow you down and just "be." Then, take a little time to simply be in His presence, and… Pray On!

My Reflections…

Week 45
Memory Care

The impact of Alzheimer's disease or other related mental diseases is intense. That fact is not new. The disease has effected most of us personally through a loved one or a close friend. Recently, I was asked to visit a memory care facility that cares for people impacted by this disease. As in other entries in this book, initially, I was uncertain what I could do or say that would help. I asked myself what would be relevant. I came back to the simple instruction that I was given which was to go to my prayer crosses and simply show that I care.

As I went down the halls of this beautifully decorated and well-staffed facility, I made eye contact with the residents. It amazed me how much could be communicated just by looking eye-to-eye with a person. As I connected with person after person that day, I handed each one of them a prayer cross. My message was short and simple. I introduced myself and told them I had a gift for them. I handed them a prayer cross. I told each person it was a visual reminder that God loved them and that He was present with them. I said that some people use the cross as a visual when they pray and that it often helped to have something to hold.

That was the entirety of most of the conversations. I left with a handshake or a brief hug. That day, I saw lots of smiles from people who simply needed to be reminded of God's love and to feel they had not been forgotten. Isn't it amazing what encouraging words and a prayer cross can do to change a life? My challenge to you this week is to take time each day to let someone know that they are loved and cared for by God Almighty and by you! Show that you care and tell others that you care, and... Pray On!

My Reflections…

Week 46
Worship Warriors

A pastor friend of mine is at a church with a very active prayer ministry. One of the things this church does that I like a lot is to use "Worship Warriors." During a worship service, in a room separate from where the worship service is going on, a person prays for the service. He or she prays for the music ministry, for the person bringing the message, and for any and all other parts of the service. At this church, during the first part of worship, people register their presence on a card that is collected. These cards are taken to the "Prayer Warrior Room" and prayed over. A space is available on each card for prayer requests. These requests are prayed over and people know that there is someone that is interceding on their behalf to God.

Recently, an addition was added to this ministry. One Sunday, the pastor talked about a prayer cross during his series on prayer. Along with the weekly prayer for the pastor, the music, and the people, a prayer cross was added to the room for the worship warriors to hold as they interceded. That cross was then given to the pastor to remind him as well as the congregation to hold on to our connection with God. It was a visual reminder to stay in a season of prayer. My challenge to you this week is to pray for your pastor and for the staff of your church. They are expected to give and give as well as to know the answers when things go wrong. They need God's guidance every single day and they need to be able to hold on to the truth that their congregation is praying for them. Pray On Warriors... Pray On!

My Reflections…

Week 47
Waiting Room

A few months after my motorcycle accident, Debbie and I were talking. We were reflecting on all that we had been through both individually and as a couple. I will never forget one thing Debbie said. She told me about the time she was in the waiting room during my two weeks of being in a coma. She spent much time with family and friends from our church in Abilene. She also became familiar with other people sitting in the same waiting area who had a loved one in critical care. She learned their stories. She celebrated news of the success and improvements with their loved ones. In time, she became close to some of her "fellow waiters" and connected to others through prayer, making the journey easier for them.

A great use of the prayer crosses I make now would be to give to people who are like my Debbie was at that time, a "waiter." You don't have to personally know each person's detailed journey in order to connect with them through prayer. Why not have your

small group at church meet once a month at the local hospital and hand out an encouraging card or a holding cross? This will serve as a reminder for those who are struggling that God is ever-present with them in their time of need. In this simple way, you are encouraging others when they may be overwhelmed and reminding them that they have a place to turn for comfort and strength. You are encouraging them to pray on. My challenge to you this week is to visit someone who is waiting on the healing of a loved one. You don't need to have a sermon prepared or know exactly what to say. Simply let them know they are loved by God and that you are there for them. Simply being reminded that we are not alone is often what the "waiters" of the world are needing. Share love, and…
Pray On!

My Reflections…

Week 48
California Fires

My cousin Kregg lives in Austin, Texas. He is a firefighter and at the writing of this devotion had been called to assist in California with a number of other firemen. This was during the time when the devastating forest fires were raging in California. I mailed him a prayer cross to remind him of God's presence and protection as he worked to save others from the fires. In an earlier devotional, I mentioned that God is always beside us, always watching over us. Even with that knowledge, people often need a gentle reminder that they are not alone. The cross was a reminder to Kregg that he had friends and family, even strangers, praying for him.

The Psalmist asks to reside in the shelter of the presence of God (Psalm 91). What a better place is there than to be in the very presence of the One who created us, loves us, and sent His Son to die for us? Praying to be in God's presence is important for all of us. Though we may face struggles or fires of our own in our daily lives, we are protected with the love of God.

Each and every day, we face emotional, spiritual, and even physical dangers on all sides. We struggle, at times, to remember that we are protected from ultimate harm by the sacrifice that Jesus made on the cross. The truth of our existence is that we are forgiven of our sins. We are nurtured and comforted by the presence of the Father. My challenge to you this week is to remember that God is ever-present. Cling to the promise given to us through the cross protects our souls, and... Pray On!

My Reflections…

Week 49
Cancer Center

Today, I did something I have wanted to do for some time. I went to a cancer treatment center where I am a former patient. As a matter of fact, one of the first prayer crosses I made was for me to hold while I went for my chemo treatments at this same center. I would sit in the chair trying to be as comfortable as one can be in hospital furniture. I would just hang on to that cross and repeat Scriptures. I'd remind myself that the Lord was right there with me. I'd say, " Okay, Jesus, you said you would not leave me or forsake me so I know You are here, even if I do not feel it, You are here".

Today, I had no agenda. I would just go up to folks I didn't know and tell them my name. I would say I came to give them a cross and to remind them that God loves them and He was here with them. That's all. Not very flashy. It was just a simple little gesture of care and a little cross to remind people of The One who cares the most!

My challenge to you is to take time in prayer to remember those battling this awful disease. Pray for them, for their families, for their friends, and for the doctors to be guided by the The Great Healer. Your prayers and presence give people hope and remind them that they are never alone and will never be forsaken by Christ. Love people who need to feel loved, and... Pray On!

My Reflections…

Week 50
Circle Drive and Wait Time

Recently, in the circle drive of my granddaughter's school , God taught me another lesson on prayer. Waiting in my pickup for her, my mind reflected on the day's activities, things accomplished, and those things yet to do. I probably sat there 10-15 minutes and then I began thinking of various family members and where they were, what they were doing, etc. Then, as I began praying for them, I thought about my prayer crosses in my console. I reached for one, holding it now as I prayed. A wonderful time of prayer followed. We often get stressed out when we have to wait in line, but that time can be seen as a blessing of time to spend with God that we might not have had otherwise.

Now, my "Circle Drive Time" has become a highly anticipated time of day for me. Instead of sitting there thinking aimless thoughts or being stressed about waiting, I can focus on things of God through prayer. I challenge you this week to inventory your day and see if there are any "Circle Drive" moments in your life that God can transform into moments to draw closer to Him through prayer. Take those times of waiting and connect with God, intercede on behalf of those in need, and simply enjoy God's presence. Never forget... Pray On !

My Reflections…

Week 51
Daily Blessing

A friend living in another city reminded me recently that I had given a family member of hers a prayer cross at one time. My friend had forgotten about it until she came across it while looking for other things to bring to their loved one. My friend told me how moved she was at seeing the cross. My friend says she was moved to be reminded of my care for a person they love. Also, she was moved to know that the cross was important to their loved one.

I was not thinking of these things when I first gave it. I simply wanted to bless someone that day. I was only thinking of that immediate moment. I am reminded that our actions today may not be fully felt until down the road. And relating to prayer, we may not experience the full impact of our prayers until later as well. Also moving is that my friend told me she brought that cross to her loved one's room and placed it on the table by their bedside knowing when they were able, they could hold it again in prayer.

My challenge to you is to practice faithfulness in the little things so that we may be blessed and be a blessing to others. Live your life as if Jesus is next to you, and... Pray On!

My Reflections…

Week 52
An Angel Among Us

I made my "beat the heat" afternoon stop today for a big cup of ice water with strawberry and lemon. This time, I went to a location that was not my normal refreshment destination. As I waited at the drive-thru window, I felt that nudge to give the worker a prayer cross. As you may remember, I had given a cross to a worker at another location and they ended up asking for a second one on another visit. Upon handing me my water, I said, "I don't know why, but I think I am supposed to give you this little cross. For me, it's just good to know that no matter what is going on, I am never alone. That's what this means to me. I sometimes hold one when I pray too." "Cool. Thanks," was her only response. I look at the worker's name tag, and I promise, the name "Angel" was on it. I see that name fairly regularly, and when I do, I am reminded of a passage in Hebrews 13:2 that tells us that we may just be entertaining one whom we think is a stranger, all the while,

159

they truly are an angel.

My purpose here is not to write a discourse on angels. All I want to do is to remind you that if you allow/ask God to direct your every step, He will put you where He wants you to be and arrange encounters with whom he wishes as well.

I believe when we live life like that, we can rest assured that He will put us in the right place at the right time. My challenge to you today is to stay open to the voice of God. Sometimes His nudging is designed to bring you assurance rather than the other person. As always... Pray On!

My Reflections…

ABOUT THE AUTHOR

Mark Phillips is an ordained minister with the United Methodist Church and has served churches in West Texas and the Texas Panhandle. He is the executive director of OvercomerNow which has a mission to turn information into inspiration. His non-profit brings in speakers who have overcome great challenges in order to inspire others to see the power of God in their own lives and to take action in moving their lives forward.

Mark is married to Debbie and they live in Amarillo, TX. Their daughters are now grown and they love the time they are able to spend with their grandchildren. Mark began giving out prayer crosses to help others and in doing so found a calling for his life that connects him with God and the people around him.

If you are interested in supporting this ministry, you can go to bit.ly/givecrosses and give a one-time donation or a monthly donation. Your support is greatly appreciated and your prayers are always greatly needed!